Original title:
Life's Meaning (I Swear It's Out There)

Copyright © 2025 Creative Arts Management OÜ
All rights reserved.

Author: Tobias Winslow
ISBN HARDBACK: 978-1-80566-219-8
ISBN PAPERBACK: 978-1-80566-514-4

## **In the Garden of Possibilities**

In the garden where dreams sprout,
Bumblebees gossip, no room for doubt.
We plant our hopes with a giggling grin,
Wishing for flowers, let the fun begin!

Watering thoughts with a dash of cheer,
We weed out worries that seem to adhere.
Sunshine laughs as we dance in the dew,
Chasing the butterflies, who knew we flew?

Each blossom whispers secrets to those,
Who pause and ponder where the wild rose grows.
A gardener's tool is a smile and a jest,
Digging for laughter, we're really quite blessed!

So here in the patch of zany delight,
We harvest the moments, till day turns to night.
With radishes sprouting and carrots in rows,
We'll toast with our shovels, for joy's what we chose!

## **Threads of Destiny Unraveled**

In the loom of our antics, threads mix and spin,
Fates twist like pretzels, where do we begin?
Pulling on fibers we've tangled with glee,
Who knew our existence was just a grand spree?

Each stitch is a laugh, a quirk or a quip,
As we weave through the chaos, we stumble, we trip.
Yet every mishap just adds to the flair,
We're crafting a tapestry, filled with rare air!

The colors of mishaps splash bright on our soul,
Yellow for laughter, and green for our goal.
So let's tug at the threads, let's see where it leads,
Chasing the rabbit, we're planting our seeds!

In a fabric of folly, we each have our place,
Piecing together, with style and with grace.
So raise up your scissors, let's snip with delight,
To a world that's stitched up, where all seems just right!

## The Language of Lost Connections

In a world of buzzing phones,
We text but feel alone.
Emoji hearts, not quite real,
Human hugs are the best deal.

Messages sent with a smile,
Lost in the cyber jungle style.
Wi-Fi signals break my heart,
Connection woes, a true fine art.

Filter fails on my selfie pic,
Trying to look young and slick.
But nothing beats a laugh and grin,
With hugs that start where words begin.

As I scroll and swipe away,
I search for joy in every way.
Yet in my quest for what's profound,
I find the fun in lost and found.

## Kaleidoscope of Hopes

Life's a twist in various hues,
Dreams chew gum with silly shoes.
Chasing rainbows on a bus,
Finding gold in each of us.

Balloon animals in the park,
Silly antics when it's dark.
Expectations float like kites,
But hope shines through, oh what sights!

Laughter bubbles, a joyful sound,
Chasing wishes that abound.
Even when the path is bent,
Frogs and fairies, no lament!

In a whirl of chance and fate,
We stumble, giggle, celebrate.
With each turn, a new delight,
A dance with shadows, pure and bright.

## Tales from the Edge of Tomorrow

Time travelers in mismatched socks,
In search of treasure, dodging rocks.
They laugh at future's tangled mess,
Juggling dreams and hopelessness.

Wink at fate and take a bow,
Prepping meals, yet dreaming how.
To toast at night, with silly cheer,
When tomorrow's worries feel so near.

In the rocket of today, we fly,
Fuelled by hopes that reach the sky.
With every bump, a bubble bursts,
But joy is what quenches our thirsts.

So let's wear our quirkiest hats,
Dance with cats, avoid the rats.
On this edge, we barrel through,
Tomorrow's tales are funny too.

# A Symphony of Unspoken Thoughts

Whispers play a gentle tune,
Laughter dances beneath the moon.
Words float by like cotton candy,
Spinning tales both bright and dandy.

The silence sings in funny ways,
Drawing smiles on rainy days.
With every pause, a giggle waits,
In the chaos, joy creates.

Secrets shared with clumsy grace,
Life's a game, a silly race.
In the echo of a laugh's embrace,
Unspoken truths find their place.

So here's to all the laughs we keep,
In the corners where shadows creep.
With every note, let's boldly quoth,
A symphony of unspoken thoughts.

## When Dreams Paint Reality

In a world where socks are mismatched,
And cats run meetings with a catch,
Chasing dreams through mud and glue,
We laugh at clouds that say "Boo-hoo!"

Every sandwich talks with flair,
Wishes ride on a purple bear,
Chasing after a rainbow's end,
Finding silly in every bend.

## Illumination in the Dark

Why do shadows dance and sway?
Catch the moon and shout, "Hooray!"
Light bulbs giggle when they flicker,
While coffee mugs start to snicker.

A spoon once declared it was a fork,
In the pantry, they all just talk,
Mixing dreams with butter and bread,
Turning thoughts into shapes instead.

## Rivers of Reflection

Wading through puddles, thoughts galore,
Fish in tuxedos, they explore,
Dancing leaves sing a tune so sweet,
While ants throw parties on tiny feet.

With every splash, a giggle's born,
As daisies plot to spring and adorn,
Riding waves of silly delight,
Where shadows play peek-a-boo at night.

## Lighthouses on Stormy Seas

Through storms that laugh like cheeky kids,
Lighthouses hold their frothy bids,
Guiding boats with beams so bright,
While seagulls crack jokes in flight.

Every wave wears a wacky hat,
Tickling whales while they chat,
Finding humor in the spray,
Sailing smiles on a wild array.

## Threads of Serendipity

In a world of mismatched socks,
We search for answers in the clocks.
Chasing cats who flee our grasp,
Finding wisdom in a rasp.

Like a pizza lost in space,
The universe laughs at our pace.
Jumbled thoughts and funny signs,
Treasure hunts for peace of minds.

Laughter spills from every cup,
As we try to figure up.
Running circles, what a game!
Our hearts dance while we proclaim.

So embrace the quirks that roam,
In this chaos, we find home.
With each twist and silly turn,
Serendipity is our learn.

## Echoing Down the Corridors

Down the halls of echo's grace,
We stumble on in a silly race.
Whispers bounce on laughter's beat,
Searching for a snack to eat.

Funny echoes, jokes on loop,
In a hall of the playful group.
Chasing dreams on rubber bands,
In a world of wobbly stands.

Tick-tock goes our feisty quest,
Finding joy, we jest the best.
A game of tag with thoughts so bright,
In the corridors, we take flight.

So let the echoes take their stand,
With giggles shared, hand in hand.
Through every twist, we'll often find,
The punchlines that make life unblind.

## Cracks in the Facade

Behind the masks, we all do play,
Hiding smiles in a funny way.
Cracks appear, the laughter spills,
As we dance on with our thrills.

Life is just a silly show,
Where the best jokes often flow.
In the glass, our dreams reflect,
With every slip, we reconnect.

So when we fall, let's laugh it off,
Join the chorus, let's cough-cough!
Through the gaps, we learn to see,
That joy persists in you and me.

Embrace the quirks, lift the veil,
In the cracks, our spirits sail.
Every flaw adds to the spice,
In this adventure, how nice!

## Melodies of Meaning

Tunes of laughter fill the air,
With quirky rhythms everywhere.
Dancing notes, a silly sound,
In this music, joy is found.

We hum through life, a cheeky beat,
With every stumble, we repeat.
Finding melodies in our blunders,
In each misstep, we have wonders.

So grab your spoons, let's make a jam,
Mixing rhythms, who gives a damn?
In the cacophony, we cheer,
Singing loud, with no fear.

Jokes and joy, the sweetest chords,
Strumming laughs with silly words.
When focus fades, just start to play,
In the music, we find our way.

## Shadows of Intent

In the shadows where I stand,
I trip over dreams, unplanned.
A squirrel mocks me from a tree,
As I ponder, what could be.

With every step, a new disguise,
I wear my socks as mittens, guys!
Chasing fortunes down the street,
Finding wisdom in bad tweets.

A fleeting thought flies past my head,
Like all my plans that soon have fled.
I swear the world's an inside joke,
Where punchlines dangle, half bespoke.

So here I stand, a clown at best,
In this circus of a quest.
With laughter echoing from the park,
I'll dance alone, embracing spark.

## Echoes of the Heart

I hear the echoes of my snacks,
In cupboards that hide their secrets back.
Whispers of cookies, chips, and pie,
They taunt me with their sugary sigh.

The heart beats on, a steady drum,
While I search for the next sweet crumb.
But every bite brings endless woes,
As pants grow tighter, goodness knows!

Yet joy resides in every crunch,
In puddles where I dive and munch.
So what if calories dance around?
I'll laugh in the chaos I have found.

With echoes bouncing off the walls,
I consider, do I hear the calls?
Of life's absurdity, sheer delight,
A comedy played in day and night.

## Searching for Light in the Dark

I stumble through the midnight haze,
Chasing shadows, lost in a maze.
The moon is hiding, playing tricks,
While I'm tangled in my own mix.

With flashlight beams that dance and sway,
I wonder what's planned for the day.
Is there a treasure just ahead?
Or is it just my bed instead?

I bump my knee, oh what a sight,
The dark reveals my inner fright.
But laughter bubbles from within,
As I navigate this silly sin.

So here I am, embracing fright,
Finding humor in the night.
For with each laugh, a spark ignites,
Illuminating all my plights.

## Threads of a Woven Journey

With threads so bright, I stitch my way,
Through fabrics of folly and dismay.
Each knot a tale, each loop a laugh,
In this tapestry, I find my path.

The loom of life, so vast and wide,
Wobbles often, like a bumpy ride.
But every twist and turn I take,
Creates the stories I will make.

Some patterns clash, some colors blend,
In this grand quilt, there's no end.
So grab your needles, come join the fun,
We'll weave our dreams until we're done!

In threads of joy, with laughter spun,
Our journey dances, never done.
So here we laugh, let worries part,
Stitched tightly with a merry heart.

## **When Stars Align**

At times I wonder, where's my spark?
With socks mismatched, I wander the park.
The universe grins, it winks with glee,
As pigeons plot the course for me.

I stumble on dreams, all jumbled and odd,
Like finding a fortune in a hotdog.
Stars laugh at my plans, a cosmic jest,
Saying, 'Just chill, you're doing your best!'

When planets collide, I trip on a shoe,
The cookies I bake resemble a zoo.
Yet somehow in chaos, joy finds its way,
A puzzle unwrapped, on a cloudy day.

So, here I stand, a jester divine,
With lemonade spills, and dance moves in line.
The stars might align, but it's quite a show,
With punchlines of fate, and comedy flow.

## **Ripple Effects**

A pebble drops in a pond so wide,
Creating circles, I take in stride.
One laugh leads to joy, a chain reaction,
Like misplacing my keys, oh, the distraction!

From awkward moments in grocery aisles,
To funny faces that make me smile.
Each giggle echoes, tiny waves expand,
In the ocean of quirkiness, all unplanned.

Spilled coffee leads to laughter galore,
As clumsy folks dance right out the door.
Tiny ripples shake up the mundane,
Turning a frown into wacky champagne.

So here's to the goofs, each messy regret,
For in these moments, joy's firmly set.
A ripple cascades, an effect so grand,
In the silliness of life, together we stand.

## Where Fate Meets Free Will

I flipped a coin, what's the deal?
Heads for pancakes, tails for the wheel.
Yet fate chuckles, a prankster so sly,
As I land on toast, oh, the reason why!

At crossroads of choices, I twirl and dance,
With a smoothie in hand, let's take a chance.
But what if the universe just plays coy?
And wraps every decision in a big ol' toy?

Free will's a jester, throwing pies in the face,
While destiny watches, a curious grace.
Each choice I make feels hilariously real,
Like ordering fries but dreaming of a meal.

So here's to the chaos, the twists and the bends,
Like socks in the dryer, that never quite blends.
In the dance of the cosmos, I twirl and I sway,
With giggles and grins, it leads the way.

## Portraits of Experience

I once knew a cat with a knack for finesse,
Painting the walls in a glorious mess.
Each paw print a canvas, a work of delight,
A masterpiece born from a feline's plight.

There's wisdom in falling, a trip on the rug,
Like stepping on gum, oh, the perfect mug!
Each blunder becomes a flicker of art,
As I navigate life, stubborn and smart.

With brushes of laughter, I color my days,
In the gallery of blunders, I lose my way.
Each wild adventure, a new stroke of fate,
With colors that shimmer, I shake off the weight.

So here's to the portraits, both funny and odd,
Where memories are splashes, a little abroad.
In the story of me, art's always at play,
With chuckles and smiles to brighten the way.

## Breaths of Hope

In a world where socks disappear,
We search for answers, year by year.
A cat on a keyboard, typing slow,
Says to us, 'Just take it slow.'

The toast falls butter-side down,
Yet smiles abound in every town.
We laugh at woes, dance in the rain,
Finding joy in the mundane chain.

## The Language of the Unsung

A squirrel debates with a passing bird,
In a language that sounds quite absurd.
The two swap stories of quests and snacks,
While dodging the neighbor's scary little Pax.

Jellybeans fall from the sky,
Hopes are planted, oh me, oh my!
They sprout into thoughts, some silly, some wise,
Like why do we always misplace our ties?

## **Tides of Discovery**

In the kitchen, a battle ensues,
Between pots and pans, making good news.
An apron flaps like a superhero's cape,
As burnt toast attempts a great escape.

The ocean whispers secrets in waves,
While we dig for shells, pretending to be brave.
The sand crabs dance, with cringes and glee,
Reminding us all, we're wild and free.

## Reflections in a Broken Mirror

A mirror cracked tells tales of old,
Of laughter and mishaps, brave and bold.
With one eye winking, the other frowns,
It captures the essence of all our clowns.

In puddles of rain, reflections play tricks,
With splashes of joy from kids throwing sticks.
Each drop a reminder of moments so dear,
That finding the silly is part of the cheer.

## Beneath the Mask of Routine

Every dawn begins with yawns,
Coffee spills, and sock decoys.
The treadmill's pause—a poignant sigh,
As I sprint in place, with no real joys.

To-do lists dance like joke-filled quirks,
Routines waltz along the floor.
Tick-tock whispers, what's the perk?
I'm overdue for laughter's roar.

Tasks like laundry, they fold so tight,
Yet dreams of grandeur say, "Not today!"
Let's play hide and seek with delight,
Who says chores can't lead to a buffet?

So here I track my daily grind,
A caped crusader in pajamas bright.
Underneath, a heart intertwined,
With silliness, I take my flight.

## The Mirror's Voice

In the morning light, I lean in close,
The mirror cracks a witty grin.
"You've got potential, but heaven knows,
That bedhead's where all dreams begin!"

Reflections bounce like playful jesters,
Toothpaste smirks like little pranks.
"Keep it real, forego the testers,
Your quirks deserve applause, not thanks!"

Each day's a giggle wrapped in toil,
The frown flips over, starts anew.
What's a hair product? Just a foil,
To mask the wild and let it through.

So let that glass reveal your charm,
With laughter echoing from your stance.
Who knew the truth could be so warm?
Join the madness; life's just a dance!

## Valleys of Inspiration

In valleys lush where jokes are shared,
Ideas bloom like springtime blooms.
Here, puns awaken, surprisingly bared,
Napping branches hum lively tunes.

I wandered paths of ticklish thought,
Amongst the flowers, whimsy grows.
"Don't stop now!" the daisies taught,
With every giggle, a truth bestows.

Clouds gather round; they play the fool,
Their fluffy bodies drift and sway.
Let humor be the golden rule,
In every shade, turn gray to play!

So skip the serious, embrace the jest,
In laughter, wisdom finds its mark.
In these valleys, we are blessed,
To wander bright, ignite the spark!

## Chasing Clouds of Clarity

I set my sights on cotton dreams,
With kite strings tied to my heart's refrain.
As laughter juggles with solar beams,
I chase the clouds, unleash the rain.

Every giggle steers the path I tread,
Wisdom whispers, but jesters shout.
"No weighty worries!" the sparrows said,
"Just dance like your morning's sprout!"

With thoughts afloat, I'll paint the sky,
The blue canvas welcomes each quirk.
If questions come, I'll just defy,
With shenanigans, I'll do the work.

So up I rise, a kite in flight,
On currents of giggles, I'll soar free.
What spark illuminates the night?
Together we'll laugh in harmony!

## Remnants of Forgotten Journeys

I tripped on a banana peel, oh what a sight,
Chasing dreams with sneakers, in the pale moonlight.
A map upside down, with directions to nowhere,
But laughter resounds, like the wind in my hair.

Lost in a jungle, my GPS broke,
With monkeys as guides, I'll just crack a joke.
Got snacks in my pockets, and bugs in my shoes,
Each step I take, it's more laughs than blues.

In search of a treasure where X marks the spot,
But all I found was a very old pot.
Filled with wishes from kids long before,
I tossed in a penny and danced on the floor.

Through twists and turns, I'll wander and roam,
Finding humor in chaos, I've finally found home.

## **Seeking the Hidden Echo**

What's that echoing from behind the tree?
A voice just asked if I'd like some tea!
Chasing shadows, playing hide and seek,
But I just tripped, and now my knees squeak.

In the forest of whims, with squirrels in suits,
Making small talk, while nibbling on roots.
The riddles they share, oh what a delight,
Filling my heart, with giggles and fright.

A quest for the truth, I take giant leaps,
Climbing up hills, while the ground just weeps.
With fairies on swings, and elves on the run,
I chase after laughter, oh isn't it fun?

Whispers of wisdom float on the breeze,
Between the absurd and moments to seize.
In this playful dance, with echoes I blend,
Searching for joy, my all-time best friend.

## Mosaic of Thoughts and Feelings

A patchwork of thoughts, stitched with a grin,
I tried to be deep, but I slipped in a bin.
With colors of laughter, and patterns of cheer,
Each block tells a tale, as I hold them near.

A puzzle misfit, with pieces askew,
Thoughts racing wild, like a cat in a zoo.
I asked my reflection what's wiser than gold,
It winked and replied, "Stay silly, be bold!"

In this jumbled design, where laughter is king,
With dumb little quirks, I can happily swing.
Life's not a series of heavy debates,
But a dance through the chaos, with light-hearted traits.

So I sketch out my days, one giggle at a time,
Adding vibrant hues, because laughter's prime.
In this colorful mess, I've come to believe,
The absurdity found is what we should achieve.

## **The Dance of Uncertainty**

I put my left foot in, then pulled it right back,
Steps feeling wobbly, like a train off the track.
Twisting and turning, like spaghetti on plates,
I sway with the rhythm of unlikely fates.

With a partner of doubt, I shuffle and slide,
But every misstep ignites joy inside.
The music may change, and the lights might fade,
Yet laughter remains, in every charade.

Spinning in circles, I step on my shoe,
And bump into questions like, "What's next to do?"
But uncertainties bloom like wild flowers here,
Each fumble a chance to bring friends near.

So let's dance through the chaos, and laugh through the mess,
Knowing each silly trip is a chance to confess.
Embracing the strange, our hearts open wide,
In this dance of the awkward, we'll take every stride.

## The Compass of the Soul

In a world where gnomes wear hats,
I search for wisdom in the chats.
The universe winks, what a tease,
As I chase clues through the trees.

My compass spins without a care,
Is it north or south? I swear!
I asked a squirrel, it just sighed,
So I'll follow butterflies, with pride.

Jellybeans dance on the breeze,
Do they point me towards my keys?
I swear the grass holds secret signs,
Or maybe it's just the dandelions.

So I tiptoe through the fields of thought,
Flipping pancakes I never bought.
While dodging fate's slapstick grin,
I chuckle, "How'd I get in this spin?"

## Unraveling the Mysteries

I ponder over breakfast toast,
Is logic what I really boast?
A donut smiles, I take a bite,
And wonder if it's wise or right.

The cat next door, quite an expert,
Says chasing tails is what I'm meant.
But do the socks I lose have fate
Or just hide under my chair's weight?

I try to read the morning's fog,
But it just curls around my dog.
Do pigeons gossip about my plight?
Or are they just prepping for flight?

With goofy hats and shoes askew,
I trip on dreams, but find a clue.
If laughter's key, then let me jest,
Because finding truth is like a quest!

## **A Dance with Destiny**

A tango in the grocery aisle,
With oranges and a charming smile.
I'll twirl with fate, if she'll agree,
While trying not to trip on brie.

Potatoes roll like tiny balls,
While destiny calls from the stalls.
I wink at fate, as she spins by,
Does she know I once tried to fly?

But every step feels rather fun,
A two-step with the baked mac'ron.
And though I may not catch her eye,
At least I've gotten by with pie!

So here's to dancing with delight,
In socks that don't quite fit just right.
Although the steps may lead astray,
I'll laugh my way through every day!

## In Pursuit of Significance

With a rubber chicken in my hand,
I'm questing for what few understand.
A wobbly world of whimsy calls,
While I juggle truths and popcorn balls.

A squirrel passed by, doing a jig,
Poking fun at my noble gig.
"Hey," I shouted, "lend a paw!"
He missed the cue; I just saw straw.

I sought the cosmic grocery store,
Where meaning's sold, and wisdom's lore.
But all I found were bargain bins,
Filled with last year's lost chins and spins.

So armed with snacks and silly dreams,
I follow laughter's flowing streams.
For chasing depth can be a jest,
At least the journey's quite the fest!

## Threads of Serendipity

In the chaos of socks, mismatched but proud,
A spirited dance, they leap from the crowd.
Every tumble and twist, a tale in disguise,
Finding joy in the mess, oh, what a surprise!

Spilled coffee on Monday, yet here we still stand,
Planned vacations turn sour, much like bad band.
Through giggles and blunders, we thread our own way,
Laughter's the fabric that brightens the gray.

Dancing with cats, oh, what a sight,
Twisting and turning, a clumsy delight.
Serendipity calls, with a wink and a grin,
In the tapestry of life, we always win!

So raise your glass high to the quirks that we own,
Each mishap a treasure, each moment, a stone.
With every lost shoe and unexpected fate,
We weave into wonder, and oh, isn't it great!

## Chasing Shadows of Truth

The cat thinks it's midnight, while I lose my socks,
Chasing shadows of truths, wrapped in paradox.
With a cereal bowl split upon the floor,
I ponder existence while I mop up the gore!

To find wisdom in hiccups, oh what a thrill,
Each quirky encounter, a cosmic drill.
Navigating life like it's a lost kid's map,
With a compass of giggles and the occasional flap.

Tickling my brain while the toaster explodes,
Truth hides in the crumbs, in unpredictable codes.
Every wrong turn a plot twist divine,
Finding laughter in chaos, it's all part of the line!

So come join the chase, with humor and cheer,
Embrace all the nonsense; let go of the fear.
In shadows we wander, but look for the light,
With laughter as our guide, every day feels just right!

**The Compass of the Heart**

In a world made of maps, I'm drawn to the odd,
Finding paths in the noodles, like pasta from God.
With a compass that spins, I laugh as I chart,
And treasure odd moments that tickle the heart.

Through roundabouts baffling, and GPS woe,
I follow the breadcrumbs, wherever they go.
With friends who are silly, we sail on this quest,
Finding joy in the offbeat, it's truly the best.

Like socks in a dryer, I tumble and spin,
Collecting odd nuggets, the joys found within.
So toss out the handbook, embrace all the arts,
The compass of laughter directs all our hearts!

We may float on the breeze, like leaves in the fall,
Or get stuck in the sofa, without sense at all.
With each tiny giggle, we dance hand in hand,
In this crazy adventure, we take our bold stand!

## **In Search of Sacred Moments**

In the depths of a closet, I spot something bright,
A tire swing waiting, beneath the moonlight.
With reckless abandon, I leap and I soar,
Chasing sacred moments, who could ask for more?

The toaster's a portal; it sends me to Mars,
While I munch on my toast topped with jam from the jars.

In the dance of the mundane, I find my delight,
Every wink from the universe feels tastily right.

Exploring the sofa for treasures untold,
With every lost penny, more stories unfold.
Each chuckle a chapter, each pause a sweet fate,
In this journey of giggles, I celebrate!

So here's to the moments, both silly and grand,
In the quest for the sacred, together we stand.
With laughter as our compass, we're bound to embark,
On a whimsical journey, igniting the spark!

## The Map of Our Dreams

We wander with a smile,
Seeking treasures all the while.
X marks spots on coffee stains,
On our hearts, we chart the gains.

Potholes filled with giggles bright,
Every turn a silly sight.
With a compass made of fun,
Who knew dreaming could be run?

Maps unfold in vibrant hues,
Mismatched socks and wobbly shoes.
Each detour, a laugh we share,
Juggling hopes without a care.

So grab your hat and join the spree,
Let's find the map of you and me.
Through laughter, we will trace the lines,
In this journey, joy defines.

## **Secrets Amongst the Stars**

Whispers drift on cosmic winds,
Stars chuckle at our childish sins.
In constellations, secrets hide,
A cosmic joke, our hopes collide.

Planets wobble in the night,
While we chase dreams with pure delight.
Aliens giggle as we muse,
What's the point? We can't refuse.

In our folly, brilliance glows,
Unraveling tales that no one knows.
Secret laughter fills the skies,
As we ponder, jokes arise.

From the Milky Way's embrace,
To each star, we find our place.
In a riddle, we belong,
Amongst the stars, it feels so wrong!

## **Heartbeats of Reality**

A rhythm of folly in our chest,
Pumping laughter, we feel blessed.
The heart skips when joy ignites,
In awkward moments, pure delight.

Chasing dreams with a silly dance,
A twirl, a stumble, a chance romance.
So let's play tag with our fears,
Skip along, forget the years.

With every beat, a chuckle grows,
In the mundane, whimsy flows.
Reality's just a funny show,
We clap hands, put on a glow.

So listen close to merry tunes,
As we twirl beneath the moons.
With every heartbeat, joy's revealed,
In laughter's light, we're unconcealed.

## **Beyond the Horizon of Thought**

We set sail on a sea of dreams,
Where each wave carries funny schemes.
With thoughts like kites, we soar high,
Laughing at clouds buzzing by.

To places where silliness reigns,
And sunshine dances on our brains.
The horizon winks, a playful tease,
Inviting us to dance with ease.

Beyond thoughts like popcorn kernels,
We juggle ideas with quirky swirls.
In this carnival of absurdity,
We celebrate vibrant diversity.

So take my hand, let's venture wide,
No limits here, just joyful stride.
In laughter's glow, we'll surely find,
The treasures that brighten the mind.

## **Reverberations of a Quiet Mind**

In the hush of a whisper, a thought takes a stroll,
Chasing reflections, while pondering the whole.
Socks in the dryer, a conspiracy at play,
Who knew lost laundry could brighten your day?

Coffee cups dancing, as caffeine does spark,
Ideas bounce lightly, like frogs in the dark.
A squirrel plays chess with a cat on a wall,
Laughing at secrets, that makes the heart call.

Nestled in chaos, a giggle appears,
When pondering purpose and all of our fears.
The clock ticks a riddle, with hands out of sync,
Revealing that pondering can make you rethink.

Riding the breeze, thoughts flutter and sway,
Making the mundane feel like a cabaret.
A kitten's big leap brings delight to the soul,
In this quest for the meaning, we're all on a roll!

## The Essence of Fleeting Moments

Tick-tock goes the clock, with donuts on the side,
Moments parade past, like a carnival ride.
Waffle cones crumble, with ice cream a splash,
Joy flickers brightly, then fades in a flash.

Chasing the sunrise, we trip on the dawn,
Stepping on shadows, while yawning and drawn.
A giggle erupts, from a slip on a floor,
Who knew such antics could stir up a roar?

Kites tugging at strings, like thoughts on the breeze,
Each drift and each tumble, a dance that appease.
A cat in a window, deep in a dream,
Is it searching for purpose, or just the sunbeam?

Between the big sighs, let laughter reside,
The essence of moments, we often confide.
Open your heart, let the small wonders in,
In the grand game of living, let the giggles begin!

## Signposts in the Fog

Lost in a blizzard, I mumble a prayer,
A signpost reads 'Left', but I'm going nowhere.
A flamingo in slippers strolls down the lane,
He's got no GPS, yet he feels no pain.

Clouds having tea, and laughing at rain,
The puzzle of purpose draws us back again.
Finding my socks while I ponder the stars,
Perhaps they're at peace in the quiet of Mars.

A mailbox that giggles, each letter a pun,
Life's cosmic joke, and we're all in for fun.
Flip the pancake of doubt, syrup it sweet,
With laughter and warmth, makes our journey complete.

The fog rolls like whispers, secrets held dear,
Guided by chuckles, it's crystal clear.
So let's roam the unknown, embrace what we find,
For the journey is sweeter with a whimsical mind!

## Fables of the Forgotten

In tales of old, where the mud puddles hide,
There's wisdom in giggles, and jokes that abide.
A snail on a voyage, with dreams of the sea,
Says 'slow is the way when you're chasing a glee!'

The shoe left behind, said to carry your soul,
Each wisdom that's learned is a sparkling stroll.
A riddle of laughter, the warmth of a grin,
Forgotten but cherished, let the fun begin.

Dancing umbrellas in a storm's wild embrace,
They tango with thunder, at a whimsical pace.
The moon winks knowingly, as shadows take flight,
In fables of wonders, we find pure delight.

So gather the stories, the quirks and the laughs,
They turn into treasures, like warm bubble baths.
For in the forgotten, we summon the cheer,
Juggling the moments, let's toast with a beer!

## Musings on the Human Journey

In a world of twists and bends,
We stumble around, making friends.
Searching for truths in odd places,
With mismatched socks and funny faces.

We chase our dreams like butterflies,
While stepping in pies and making sighs.
The map's a joke, but still we roam,
With ice cream cones as our true home.

Sometimes we wonder, what's the clue?
Where's the treasure hidden from view?
In laughter and chaos we might find,
The wisdom that tickles the heart and mind.

So let's toast to the trips we take,
With goofy grins and too much cake.
For every turn, a reason to cheer,
In this wacky ride, we hold so dear.

## Fables of the Unseen Path

Once upon a time in a town,
A squirrel wore a tiny crown.
He ruled the trees with nutty schemes,
While dreaming of marshmallow dreams.

The rabbits plotted day and night,
To discover their next tasty bite.
With carrots dressed in silly hats,
They danced and sang like carefree cats.

There's wisdom in the oddest tales,
Where goats ride bikes and fish wear tails.
In laughter lies the hidden spark,
That lights the way through the dark.

So gather round, let's share a grin,
With joyful tales of where we've been.
In every chuckle, a truth may gleam,
A hint of purpose in the absurd theme.

## Beyond the Veil of Ordinary

In the kitchen, pots collide,
As cats engage in a playful ride.
The dishes dance while spoons do sway,
Chaos reigns in a funny way.

Outside the jester birds sing loud,
While clouds parade like an odd crowd.
Their silly shapes bring laughter forth,
A hidden wisdom, of great worth.

In every mishap, a lesson lies,
Like when the toaster starts to rise.
With burnt toast crumbles and giggle fits,
Finding joy in the smallest bits.

So here's to the quirky, bright and bold,
And to the stories waiting to be told.
Through jests and jests, our hearts ignite,
In search of meaning, we laugh and write.

## The Silent Call of Adventure

In gardens where the gnomes conspire,
To build a rocket made of fire.
They whistle tunes that sound absurd,
As butterflies twist, and flowers stirred.

The dogs wear hats; they think they're kings,
As the cat serenades with silly strings.
Chasing shadows, they leap and bound,
In a world where fun is always found.

Under bright moons, the owls convene,
To discuss the laughter that's rarely seen.
In dreams, they plot their next great feat,
With crickets playing a jazzy beat.

So heed the call, don't sit too still,
Grab a cupcake, seek out the thrill.
In the silence of the night so clear,
Adventure whispers, "Come, my dear."

## Murmurs from the Abyss

In the depths, I hear a chuckle,
A shadow points, can it be subtle?
Meanwhile, my sock has lost its mate,
Perhaps it's searching for a fate.

The toaster's laughing, what a sight,
It burns my toast with pure delight.
The fridge hums tunes in the night,
Is that a song or just a fright?

I ponder on a peanut's tale,
In its shell, a grand detail.
Do nuts have dreams? I often muse,
Then my shoes yell, 'You've got to choose!'

So here I am, on this strange rock,
Talking to plants, they mock my clock.
With every giggle the world may share,
I find my truth in a silly affair.

## Visions in the Twilight

Dancing shadows on the wall,
Tell me secrets, however small.
A cat insists it rules the dusk,
While I seek solace in the husk.

The stars are smirking from above,
Whispering tales, all filled with love.
Why do we worry, fret, and fear?
Just watch the moon, it's always near.

With every laugh, a giggle's found,
In every stumble, joy is bound.
Like spaghetti thrown upon the floor,
Sometimes a mess can mean much more.

So here we tumble, trip, and sway,
Finding joy in the awkward play.
In the twilight, life's quirky flow,
Brings chuckles that we've yet to know.

## The Enigma of Everyday

A coffee cup, a riddle unclear,
Why does it spill? It sheds a tear.
The spoon declares, "I'm not your friend,"
And laughs as sugar comes to blend.

My sock drawer is a circus show,
When will those unmatched pairs get to go?
Pairing socks is a fine art,
But why not wear them, each a part?

The toaster's tales leave me bemused,
With every crumb, I feel confused.
Yet in the chaos, sparks of light,
Laughter blooms in the mundane fight.

Everyday puzzles tucked away,
In sleepy corners where dreams sway.
The enigma is recorded bliss,
In the absurd, a perfect kiss.

## Seeds of Reflection

Plant the seeds, what will they grow?
Maybe laughter, maybe a show.
I tossed some dreams into the air,
And watched them giggle without a care.

The sunbeams tap dance on the ground,
They whisper secrets without a sound.
While leaves debate on turning gold,
Their humor's worth more than diamonds sold.

The world spins round with silly glee,
As clouds parade all fancy-free.
Why do we fret on serious things?
When joy can wear the silliest rings?

So here we sit, and watch the fun,
Life's creeping by, a joyful run.
In every sprout, a laugh is grown,
And deep within, the truth is shown.

## Raindrops of Realization

Raindrops fall on my silly hat,
I ponder deep, while wearing that.
A pigeon coos, it seems to know,
The secrets hidden in life's flow.

I trip on thoughts, like tangled yarn,
Chasing shadows, I stop, then turn.
A blink of truth, a better way,
To laugh and dance through every fray.

With soggy shoes, I strut along,
Waltzing to a quirky song.
The puddles giggle, splashes fly,
Why so serious? I wonder why!

So gather laughter, let it bloom,
In every corner, every room.
Embrace the chaos, skip and hop,
For wisdom's sweet, and you can't stop.

## When Dreams Take Flight

I dreamt of pizza, oh what a sight,
But woke up hungry, to my delight.
I soar through clouds, on pepperoni,
   Is this a sign? Or is it phony?

Chasing wishes on butterfly wings,
   I question all the little things.
   Is there a prize for best 'Yay!'
When life's a stage and we all play?

The birds keep squawking, what do they say?
"Time to get up!" or "Sleep all day!"
I scratch my head and shine my shoes,
   A twist of fate in silly views.

With dreams like jellybeans in hand,
I leap and laugh, it's all quite grand.
So take a trip on a whim so bright,
And let your heart take joyful flight.

## The Tapestry of Existence

Threads of color weave my day,
In shades of laughter, come what may.
Stitching memories, silly and bold,
A patchwork quilt of tales retold.

A cat parade in mismatched socks,
Who knew humor came from flocks?
A twist of fate, a yarn so grand,
It tickles my heart, makes life unplanned.

We roll through life on marble floors,
Dodging chaos, opening doors.
What's the secret? Shh, don't you frown,
It's to wear a crown made of your gown.

So raise a toast to the wacky ride,
With each blunder, let fears subside.
In every stitch, let laughter dance,
Embrace with joy, let humor prance.

## **Pillars of Understanding**

I built my thoughts on wobbly chairs,
With funny quotes and silly flares.
A juggling life, I drop my pride,
As wittiness becomes my guide.

Muffins talk and toast gives cheer,
They whisper secrets that I hear.
The fruitcake laughs, it knows my quest,
To make sense of this quirky jest.

Through each stumble, I learn to grin,
A smile at loss, a laugh at sin.
For every misstep, I find my ground,
In every chuckle, truth is found.

So let's toast to the playful clash,
Of wisdom found in the silliest flash.
With pillars strong yet full of glee,
We'll dance through chaos, wild and free.

## Dreams Adrift in Time

In a land where socks get lost,
I search for purpose at all cost.
The clock is ticking, yet I stand,
With chocolate crumbs stuck on my hand.

Chasing dreams that slip like gel,
My thoughts get tangled, what the hell?
I trip on rainbows, fall through the air,
Should have worn shoes, but who can care?

A ponder here, a giggle there,
Questions sprout like grass everywhere.
With laughter loud, I dance in my room,
Is this absurdity or true bloom?

So I toast to the dreams I juggle,
With ice cream scoops and silly chuckle.
When in doubt, I'll brew some tea,
And ponder on what my fate could be.

## The Song of the Searching Heart

In the kitchen, I sing a tune,
Where spaghetti dreams swirl like a balloon.
I search for zest in a bowl of soup,
To find the rhythm, join the loop.

The cat watches me, yawns with style,
As I dance, he's judging all the while.
Should I take a trip to Neptune's shore?
Or settle for snacks and simply snore?

With each step forward, I trip and slide,
But who can rule when the fun's inside?
With twinkling eyes, I chase my fable,
Is it glorious, or just unstable?

So here I sing, loud and free,
In a world that's made for goofy glee.
With hope as my trusty guide,
Let's find the smiles that we can't hide.

## In the Shadow of Our Choices

With forks in hands, we choose our fate,
Should I have chocolate or just one plate?
Each decision strikes my silly mind,
Like socks that never seem to bind.

Am I a dreamer or just unclear?
As choices loom, I sip my beer.
A twist of lemon, a splash of grace,
I smile at odds that I can't replace.

In buffet lines of hopes and fears,
I grab a fortune cookie, cheers!
It splits and reveals my clumsy path,
But all it says is "Take a bath."

So here I dance, a brave ballet,
In shadows long, I joke and play.
With laughter echoing, pure delight,
I find the joy in endless night.

## The Garden of Infinite Questions

Welcome to the garden of my mind,
Where weeds grow wild and thoughts unwind.
I plant the seeds of joy and fear,
With silly phrases that volunteers hear.

What if ducks could skate on ice?
Or pizza had a veggie slice?
With butterflies whispering in my ear,
I chase the sun, and sip my beer.

A gnome pops up, wearing a hat,
He wants to know what's up with that.
With petals swirling all around,
I toss a question, see what's found.

So if you wander in this space,
Prepare to laugh, and find your place.
Among the blooms, just stop and stare,
You might just find a little flair.

# Labyrinth of Hearts

In a maze of thoughts, we roam and play,
Chasing shadows that dance and sway.
With every turn, a giggle escapes,
Oh, where's the exit? Who makes the maps?

We stumble on love, like socks in a drawer,
The heart's a jigsaw, missing pieces galore.
But isn't it funny how we all just grin?
Searching for meaning, let the chaos begin!

Curly paths lead to a donut shop,
While pondering life, can't we just stop?
A cup of coffee or a slice of pie,
Maybe that's wisdom in dessert's sweet lie!

So twirl in the maze, chase your own tail,
Wrap up the laughter, set sail on this trail.
For all that we seek in the paths that we choose,
Is often just joy, with a sprinkle of blues.

## **Ink on the Pages of Time**

With scribbles and doodles, we write our tale,
On napkins, on walls, with a cup, we prevail.
Every day's story a little absurd,
Like a chicken who thinks she can fly like a bird!

Erasers are scared of our dramatic flair,
As we scribble our dreams without any care.
Each line is a giggle, a faint memory,
Of a day that was wild, or maybe just me.

The ink spills secrets like coffee on shoes,
Making our moments a colorful muse.
Pages full of laughter, pages full of sighs,
So let's toast to the mess, with pie in our eyes!

As we flip through the chapters, let's dance in the rain,
Celebrate the chaos, embrace all the sane.
For in these wild prints, our hearts will align,
Painting the canvas, one line at a time!

## The Heart's Compass

My heart has a compass, but it's a bit cracked,
It points to the fridge when I'm needing a snack.
I'm lost in the woods, yet I bask in the sun,
Taking wrong turns, but boy, wasn't it fun?

It beeps when I'm hungry, and chirps when I roam,
A quest for the tacos, a search for my phone.
With every misstep, a laugh comes to play,
As I navigate life in my clumsy ballet.

Oh compass of hearts, what riddles you weave,
Promising treasures we seldom conceive.
Might it be friendship, or a pizza slice hot?
Perhaps it's the laughter we find in the knots.

So I'll follow the needle wherever it spins,
To discover the joy that each adventure wins.
In the grand scheme of things, let's not take a pause,
As we wander this world, just because!

## **Where Questions Lie**

In corners of doubt, the questions will hide,
Like socks in the dryer, no clue where they bide.
With coffee in hand, I ponder and muse,
While the cat chases shadows, oh what to choose?

Do I fry eggs or just have a toast?
Is existence a joke or a heavenly boast?
While stars twirl above, I chuckle and grin,
Maybe the answers lie somewhere within.

From pigeons to pancakes, the world's quite absurd,
Like a philosophical chicken that never gets heard.
Unravel the puzzle with humor and cheer,
For the punchline of life's just a wink and a beer!

So let's toast to the questions, and dance in delight,
With confetti of laughter, we'll brave the night.
As we wander through wonders, let worries comply,
For the mystery's sweet, where the questions lie!

## **Embers of Insight**

In the kitchen of dreams, we bake a pie,
Mixing hopes with laughter, oh me, oh my!
Ingredients of whimsy, a sprinkle of wit,
Slicing through the silence, each crumb a hit.

The cat steals a bite, then jumps in surprise,
While the toaster sings sonnets under bright skies.
We trade silly glances, a feast made of fun,
Life's little moments, oh how they run!

A dance with the shadows, chasing our tails,
With socks on our hands, oh, how the fun prevails!
We giggle like children, unhinged by the day,
Finding joy in the silly, in every odd way.

So raise your glass high, let's toast to the jest,
For in laughter we find what we love the best.
Embers of insight, glowing warm in our hearts,
In the humor of chaos, that's where it starts.

### **Sails in the Storm**

Upon the sea of questions, we sail askew,
With a compass of chuckles, we're never blue.
Waves crash with sarcasm, the wind howls a tune,
As we dance with the dolphins beneath the full moon.

With a parrot on our shoulder, we shout, 'Avast!'
Steering through the nonsense, sails flying fast.
The ship's full of pirates, all jolly and bold,
As we navigate life's treasures, never growing old.

Buckets of merriment, tossed over the side,
Seagulls squawking laughter, on this adventurous ride.
Through storms of confusion, we hoot and we holler,
Sails in the tempest, our spirits grow taller.

So here's to the swashbucklers, brave and bizarre,
Finding gold in the shadows, our own guiding star.
In the wild winds of whimsy, we chart our own course,
Laughing through the squalls, with insatiable force.

# A Symphony of Echoes

In the concert of chaos, we dance, we sway,
Notes made of giggles are here to stay.
With kazoo in hand, we conduct a parade,
As the world joins in, a laugh serenade.

The echo of chuckles fills the grand hall,
Bouncing off the walls, we stand tall.
With each unexpected note, our spirits lift high,
Creating a symphony that can't say goodbye.

A trumpet of wisdom, a xylophone of cheer,
The melody of madness is loud and sincere.
In the mix of it all, we find our sweet zone,
Each chord a reminder, we're never alone.

So let's play this music, in harmony blend,
For in laughter's embrace, we always transcend.
A symphony of echoes, in every heart's beat,
Finding joy in the chaos, where life feels complete.

## Ascending the Ladder of Wonder

With a ladder of dreams, we climb up so high,
Each rung painted bright with a whimsical sky.
Up we go giggling, like children at play,
As we reach for the stars in a curious way.

A curious monkey swings from the top,
Dropping ripe bananas, oh plop, plop, plop!
With every small slip, we laugh and we cheer,
For mistakes make the journey much brighter, I hear.

The view from the top shows the silliness spread,
With castles of fluff, where no worry is bred.
We wave to the clouds, invite them for tea,
On the ladder of wonder, we're wild and free.

So let's climb ever higher, no fear in our hearts,
For each step taken gives joy that imparts.
Ascending together, from giggles to glee,
In the wondrous adventures, we're happy to be.

## Whispers of Purpose

In a world filled with quirks, we explore,
Chasing tales like children, always wanting more.
Each step a giggle, each stumble a cheer,
With every odd moment, the end feels so near.

We stop for a snack, a writer's block muse,
With peanut butter dreams, and chocolate to use.
A search for the punchline, a tickle from fate,
In this grand cosmic joke, we celebrate late.

With shadows that dance in the town square's light,
We trade our deep thoughts for a silly kite flight.
Beneath the big sky, our laughter takes wing,
In the silence of stars, hear the fun that we bring.

Each misstep a marker, each joy like a crown,
In pursuit of the silly, we never back down.
Together we gather the moments in glee,
As whispers of purpose tickle you and me.

## The Quest for Each Dawn

With mornings that giggle and coffee that sings,
We seek out the dumbest of magical things.
Like socks that don't match, or a cat with a bow,
Our quest grows absurd, but who cares? Let's go!

We chase after sunlight, our shadows behind,
With laughter like echoes, sweet madness combined.
A squirrel on a quest, relentless as fate,
Joins in on our fun; oh, is this a date?

We dance with the daisies, do cartwheels on grass,
While time tickles past us; we're just having sass.
In the mundane absurd, we find our delight,
For every new dawn, we'll do it just right.

With forks in the road, choices made on a whim,
We taste every flavor, our future not dim.
Crack jokes with the trees, and laugh with the breeze,
In this vibrant adventure, we're always at ease.

## Echoes of Existence

Among the clatter of forks and a plate,
We muse on our answers while munching on fate.
With faces like puzzles and voices like drums,
We echo the laughter — if anyone comes!

In hallways of thoughts where the weirdest reside,
Abundant in quirks, we snack side by side.
As breadcrumbs to freedom, our giggles will lead,
To moments of wisdom, like ice cream, we need.

We seek the absurd in the fabric of time,
With a wink and a pun, everything's primed.
So stick with the path where the odd filters flow,
In socks that don't match, let your heart freely go.

Each moment a jest, like clowns on parade,
We dance through our troubles, together unafraid.
As echoes of existence dance through the air,
We revel in joy, strip confusion with care.

## Beneath the Stars We Wander

With giggles and snacks, we roam through the night,
Chasing shooting stars in our pajamas so bright.
We ask the moon questions, giggling in glee,
"Do you know the secrets? Come play hide-and-seek!"

As constellations wiggle in playful display,
We sketch out our dreams in a whimsical way.
Like turtles on surfboards and fish in a tree,
We celebrate oddness, all wild and free.

The cosmos our canvas, each wish a stroke bold,
In laughter and wonder, our stories unfold.
With quirks and with quirks, we embrace the absurd,
In each twinkle of starlight, our laughter's the word.

So let's wander together through this night of delight,
With sheep made of marshmallows, on journeys we'll write.
Amongst cosmic confetti, let joy be our guide,
As we seek out the silly, with nothing to hide.

## The Art of Being

In a world full of chaos and noise,
We stumble and fumble like kids with toys.
Chasing our tails, we laugh and we spin,
Finding the joy in our quirky skin.

With breadcrumbs of dreams scattered along,
We sing silly songs, our lives a fun song.
Each hiccup and stumble becomes our dance,
Making the mundane a charming romance.

The wise ones say, 'Just follow your heart,'
But mine seems to lead to a thrift store cart.
Where socks become hats and spoons sing at night,
In this wacky circus, everything feels right.

So here's to the strays who dare to be free,
Creating a life that's just like a spree.
With vibrant confetti and laughter so loud,
We're the fabulous oddballs, proud of our crowd.

## Silent Whispers of the Ages

The clock ticks, but aren't we all late?
In a race for the cheese on our tiny plate.
We ponder the deep as we sip our tea,
What ancient sage knew what chips would be free?

The ghosts of our past try to share their tales,
But they trip over rocks and stumble on rails.
In whispering winds, do they chuckle or frown,
As we wear our blame like an old, worn-out crown?

With every lost sock, a new mystery grows,
Like where did my pen go? No one really knows.
These silent musings through the laughter we share,
Uncovering the wonder in mishaps laid bare.

So we take to the streets, our thoughts turned to fun,
Chasing after moments just shimmering in sun.
May the legends of laughter echo so clear,
Each chuckle a saga we hold very dear.

## Colors of Existence

In a box full of crayons, pick your own hue,
Mix oranges with blues, see what comes true.
Splash your life canvas with giggles and flair,
For who needs perfection when chaos is there?

Oh, the shades of existence, they wobble and sway,
Like a cat in a hat doing ballet today.
Each brushstroke a memory, however absurd,
From pancake brunches to the chirp of a bird.

Dancing through puddles in gumboots so bright,
The colors of joy are a glorious sight.
A canvas alive with all kinds of fun,
Who needs a gather to speak of what's won?

So here's to the whirl of life's vibrant styles,
In rainbow hues, let's embrace all the wiles.
With laughter as pigment, we paint the unknown,
Creating a masterpiece uniquely our own.

## Journeys into the Unseen

We set sail on a ship made of jellybeans,
With seats upholstered in old magazines.
Charting a course through the skies up high,
As candy clouds float and giggles ne'er die.

The map is a riddle, the compass confused,
But laughter's the treasure that's never refused.
Beyond all the normal, we leap and we spin,
Where questions are answered by grins on a whim.

Each twist of fate, like a quirky old toy,
Sparking adventures, igniting pure joy.
In lands where the odd is the beauty's own crown,
We twirl through the shadows, never wearing a frown.

So pack up your bags, the odd and absurd,
Let's gather our quirks like a riotous bird.
For in every strange journey, with laughter we lean,
We find that the unseen is beautifully keen.

www.ingramcontent.com/pod-product-compliance
Lightning Source LLC
Chambersburg PA
CBHW070749220426
43209CB00083B/194